UPWARD

Seven Secrets from my Chocolate Lab for Having an Awesome Life

Also by Edward Vilga

Yoga in Bed

Yoga for Suits

Acting Now

UPWARD DOG

Seven Secrets from my Chocolate Lab for Having an Awesome Life

by Edward Vilga

**All knowledge,
the totality of all questions and answers,
is contained in the dog.**
—Franz Kafka, *Investigations of a Dog*

Dedicated to man's — and very specifically my — best friend...

BELLE'S SEVEN SECRETS

INTRODUCTION

The most successful individual I know is currently sleeping blissfully at my feet.

She's also the happiest and the most self-actualized being I've ever met.

And, like all truly great teachers, she instructs almost entirely by example.

To be honest with you, although I've trained extensively and been teaching yoga for over a decade, no Sanskrit scroll or mountaintop guru has taught me nearly as much about life as Belle, my chocolate lab, does during a single hike. In fact, for a while now, my chocolate lab has been a model for me of "how to be" in the world.

You see, for many years I've taught some of the most physically challenging yoga classes in New York City and Los Angeles. Pretty soon though, once you get your foot behind your head, you find yourself asking "So what?... Is any of this making my life any better? Sure, I'm more flexible, but am I really any happier?"

When I started looking around for the next set of answers, I realized that what I really wanted was to have the same incredible attitude towards life that Belle has.

Living joyfully in the present moment, constantly curious, exuding pure friendliness and enthusiasm that affects pretty much everyone she encounters, and most importantly, radiating an ability to let go and love unconditionally...she really is my guru (albeit one I have to walk and feed twice a day). Because Belle is aligned, grounded and connected, things flow smoothly for her. Simply put: Belle knows the secrets of having an awesome life.

The time has come where I feel compelled to share with the world seven of Belle's secrets, wisdom she offers freely with every wag of her tail.

SECRET #1
LIVE IN THE NOW
How Belle lives her life completely in the present moment

LIVE IN THE NOW

Perhaps the hardest thing to do in yoga — or in life — is to stay present. We are continually pulled towards the past and the future, rarely living in the here and now.

Once, just as I decided that the theme of my class was going to be "Staying Present," I got down on my yoga mat to practice some poses. Belle, however, just wouldn't leave me alone.

She kept nuzzling me, wanting to share her toys or play one of our games.

"Not now...Not now," I kept correcting her, growing increasingly agitated.

"Not Now...Not Now," I repeated automatically, until suddenly I started laughing. How ridiculously ironic that while prepping a class about "Staying Present" all I could do was repeat "Not Now!"

The very first verse of the yoga Sutras — texts that are at least a few thousand years old — reads "Now begins the study of yoga."

Far more than a rhetorical device like "Once Upon A Time," this "Now" has important meaning: we're instructed that the wisdom we need is available to us Right Here and Right Now. The school for getting wise about our lives doesn't have a Fall or Spring Term; the practice starts at this exact minute (if we let it).

That's why this Secret — LIVE IN THE NOW — is the foundation of all Belle has to teach us. Not only does the Now contain everything we need...ultimately it's all we really have.

PROBLEMS ONLY EXIST IN THE PAST AND FUTURE

I've had a lot of problems in my life, most of which never happened.
—Mark Twain

I can totally identify with Twain's problems which "never happened." I was raised to be a first-class worrier, trained to "sweat the small stuff." It often still feels "natural" to fuss and fret over the most mundane trivia of my life.

Belle, on the other hand, doesn't worry about anything, and frankly everything works out just fine for her.

The devil's advocate position is obvious: She's "just" a dog — what could she have to be worried about?

Well in theory, Belle could worry about tons of things. After all, she's pretty dependent on me for food, shelter, and companionship. And yet I don't think it's ever crossed her mind that I might decide to stop feeding her, much less replace her with a younger, cuter dog (as if such a thing were possible!).

Fully living in the present moment, Belle is intensely secure in all her relationships and she conducts her life from a position of total trust that all will be well.

Right now, that's definitely my biggest spiritual challenge: not worrying but trusting a little bit more each day that the universe is looking out for me.

Looking back, not only has my worrying done very little good, it's generally been about disasters that never happened.

On the broadest level — with things utterly beyond our control — we humans do manage to take some matters on faith. Even with all our environmental challenges

Not only does the Now contain everything we need...ultimately it's all we really have.

these days, we still believe that the earth will continue its orbit around the sun. We don't give much thought to how gravity keeps everything remarkably consistent, especially given that our planet is spinning in a galaxy that's moving 370 miles a second through space. When it comes to the largest questions — like whether the sun will come out every morning — we just trust that somehow, it will all be fine.

Whenever I'm feeling myself about to get frazzled by worry, I try to watch Belle's deep breathing as she naps. Breathing (in Sanskrit, *pranayama*) is so central to yoga for many reasons, but perhaps most importantly because it draws your awareness inside and into the present. Belle's deep and steady breathing always helps connect me back to the present moment, a place where most of my problems do not really exist. In the Now, all is well.

MILKING THE MOMENTS

When you finished reading a child a favorite story, he or she will invariably respond, "Again! Read it again!"

Even as a teenager, when my music collection was more limited than my current vast iTunes library, I used to do that all the time with my favorite records. I remember wearing down the vinyl albums I was most passionate about, listening to favorite tracks over and over.

I've noticed that as adults, we usually don't "milk the moment" for all the joy it contains. Our "to do" lists are so lengthy, and yet we rarely include "celebrate" on them.

Belle, however, is a genius at the art of appreciation. Invariably, whenever she's happy, she seeks out her bone. Or when someone comes over for a visit, she greets them with her treasures. When something good is happening, just as when a happy engagement is suddenly announced and everyone breaks out the champagne, Belle always finds a way to extend and amplify her enjoyment. Like a billionaire savoring his cognac and Cuban cigar, she demonstrates how to treasure every aspect of a special moment and kick things up a notch.

I often skimp on savoring my victories. I know I've achieved many goals that were inspiring and important to me, only to give myself the briefest moment to celebrate before rushing on to the next challenge.

That's why Belle sets such a good example for me. Every time I see Belle milking a moment of joy, I try to remind myself to do the same. Rather than focusing on the next mountain I need to climb (or the tiny detail that still needs fixing), I'm retraining myself to savor what's right with my world, to extend and enhance my appreciation of all that's going well. Like Belle with her bone, I want to milk, amplify, and extend the positive moments as much as I can. It just seems to be a much nicer way to live.

YOU GOTTA MOVE!

All day long, Belle reminds me of how vital it is to move. Belle wouldn't dream of setting down to sleep without elaborately adjusting and making herself comfortable. She'd never wake herself up without indulging in some luxurious "downward dogs." It's second nature to her.

Today, while we were walking through the building where I have a writer's office, Belle — who was off-leash — suddenly began running ahead and then back to me for a few completely unscheduled Victory laps, all for apparently no other purpose than that I'm sure that it felt great to sprint. More than just traveling from point A to point B, she frolics.

I realized early on that I loved challenging and athletic yoga classes for many reasons, but perhaps mostly because I have to get really present in order to participate. Rather than mentally juggling bills or overanalyzing relationships, movement allows me to zone into what's happening physically in the present moment. Otherwise, I'll be several poses behind and probably topple over. The harder the class, the more it's a vacation from my own habitual thought stream.

You can apply this to almost any absorbing physical activity, from marathon running to ballroom dancing to golf. Whether we know it or not, part of the joy we obtain from participating comes in our retreat from the past and the future and return to the present.

Nowadays when I'm teaching yoga, the bulk of my instruction is about encouraging self-awareness. I used to care more about getting people into "correct" shapes but don't so much anymore. A student's internal awareness matters so much more than someone else's definition of "perfect form."

Unlike Belle, I need physical challenges to bring me back to body awareness. She's taught me to focus on what's happening right in front of me. Rather than missing out on my life, I want to treasure it just as it's happening, moment by present moment.

THE POWER OF BEING PRESENT: JUST LISTEN

Just down the street, there's a sweet, slow, burly old dog named Shadow who's about 13 (91 in human years). Shadow loves Belle and always picks up his step a bit to greet her. Shadow's retiree owner Hannah even jokes that Belle is Shadow's girlfriend.

Although he is in his 90's, Shadow's still an animal therapy dog who works with the ASPCA. (Inspired by Shadow, Belle was certified last month.) Hannah told me a horrific story that was all over the local news last year about an eight year-old boy who was so violently abused and covered with burns that even after he was rescued and his parents placed in jail, he wouldn't speak and didn't appear to understand anything that was said to him. His doctors honestly didn't know if he was suffering from brain damage or had simply decided to entirely tune out the world.

The major breakthrough occurred when the boy's doctors began to suspect he was communicating with Shadow when he and the dog were by themselves in the playroom. The boy appeared to be making some kind of sounds whenever he would hug Shadow and cling to his fur. Or Shadow would lie down and let the boy gently drip marbles into his ear, and then the boy would seem to whisper something inaudible.

The doctors strapped a small microphone on Shadow's collar and learned that not only was the boy talking to Shadow, but when they were left alone he was also reading to him. No therapist — however well-trained or well-meant — could have created the simple level of trust that Shadow achieved "just" by being present for the boy.

About a decade ago, I volunteered to mentor a homeless

Being present and appreciating someone is worth more than 10,000 pep talks.

kid whom I quickly grew to love like a little brother. Tyrone was kicked out of his family home in Antigua at 13 when they found out he was gay, and he'd been drifting around ever since. Carrying around Nietzsche and Whitman as his free reading on the NYC subways, at 17 Tyrone was an incredibly smart kid, who under other circumstances, would have been in college, perhaps majoring in Comparative Literature or Philosophy. Instead he was wandering in and out of various foster programs, clashing with authority or simply "forgetting" the rules and curfews.

Almost every offer of practical assistance I made to Ty pretty much blew up in my face. Grateful for an emergency loan, Ty would say he was only a 20 minute walk away and heading right over and yet hours later he still wouldn't have shown up. When he was threatened with getting kicked out of his foster program unless he found a part-time job but was having trouble finding one without a way of being reachable for messages, I got him a voicemail account. After about two days, he stopped checking messages until his voicemail was so full you couldn't even leave one. Time and again, I thought I was helping him in the most practical, no-strings-attached, "teach a man to fish" ways and yet nothing was working.

Frustrated, I finally confided in the head of his program. She explained to me that it was definitely not my job to fix anything in Ty's life. My most important — in fact my ONLY — job was simply to "be there" for him.

After so many in Ty's own family had rejected him and since most of the people he knew from the street were at best, completely transitory, fleeting party-friends if not outright users, his knowing that I'd somehow be present for him meant everything. Even if he didn't call me for weeks, years later (after he'd gotten into college) Ty said just knowing that I was there if he needed me, made all the difference.

I try to remember all of this whenever I feel the temptation to fix anyone's life. Even yesterday when an old friend sent me a dismal email the day after a milestone birthday lamenting the last three "wasted" decades of her life, I fought back the impulse to offer lots of constructive suggestions. I finally get that it wouldn't have been the least bit helpful. Instead, I practiced NOT advising or trying to artificially elevate her mood, but just being there for her as a loving presence.

What Shadow and Belle have mastered, and I'm trying to learn, is that my authentically paying attention is really all that's important. It's not any advice I give or any bonding over injustices. It's neither buying into a sense of victimhood nor finding the practical solution to anyone's woes.

Belle and Shadow demonstrate that just being present and appreciating someone is worth more than 10,000 pep talks.

FOCUS ON THE STICK

Belle is the friendliest dog in the world, but friendly in the dog world means she wants to growl and run and chase after every fun-looking dog she spies.

On our hikes, I can usually spot the behavior before it happens. It will always be after she spies a dog

somewhere around her size, age, and temperament. There is a certain slowing down of her gait as she makes her decision to engage. Suddenly, she charges towards the other dog with high hopes of fun.

Almost always, the dogs are totally OK with this behavior. It's only the dog owners who get startled by her mock growl and pounce. More and more, I find myself "pre-apologizing" for anything that might happen on our hikes. "She's totally friendly but sometimes she barks," I'll call out loudly as Belle scopes out a potential playmate, hoping that my preemptive disclaimer will cover any loud noises or rambunctious play.

I experimented briefly with keeping Belle on her leash for the entire hike, but frankly that's so much less fun for her and it feels almost like I'm punishing her for wanting to have a good time.

Then one day, I hit upon the perfect antidote. Now from the moment we get out of the car and I produce her favorite stick from the trunk, Belle's on the job. She is determined to carry her stick in her mouth for the entire hike. Completely absorbed in her concentration, Belle would never dream of abandoning her stick to chase another dog. Simply put, she is a dog with a mission.

Now she gets over a dozen smiles and compliments each and every time we visit Runyon Canyon from hikers who are amused and impressed with her diligence and swagger with her treasure. "It's an important job," I tell passersby who compliment her, which is obvious in the enormous pride and joy Belle radiates in her task.

In the end, like most powerful solutions, it's extraordinarily simple. My problems were instantly and completely solved once I realized it's all about focus — in this case, focus on a ten-inch piece of oak. Having that stick at the ready has transformed our hikes from worrisome, apology-filled treks to totally enjoyable, even purpose-filled adventures.

The yoga sutras explain that **"The practice of concentration on a single subject is the best way to make the mind one-pointed."** *(Sutra 1:32)* Making the mind "one-pointed" allows an extremely wide definition of what we could consider "meditation." That's why you can sit there and watch your breath, or chant the same mantra or phrase, or pray the rosary, or even savor the nuances of walking, and still technically be meditating.

Focusing on the stick is the way that works for Belle. Give her one compelling thing to concentrate on, and she shuts everything else out. There's nothing remarkable in this tiny piece of wood, but somehow it has become my magic wand to make Belle totally "One-Pointed." Absolutely nothing is more important to her than her mission with the stick, and everything else just fades into the background.

I try to remember this lesson all the time. Although I'm not literally pouncing on every distraction I encounter during my day, quite frankly my mind usually is. That's why meditating is such a valuable discipline: It's the best way I know to train myself to focus, something that requires being present, Here and Now, which when it comes to having an awesome life, really is the vital first step.

HAVE FUN

Belle not only reveals the true purpose of our existence, she also lives it 100%

ONE RULE

Belle has a worldview that pretty much defines her entire existence: Life is meant for having fun.

In his poem *One Rule,* the great 15th century Sufi mystic Hafiz put it this way:

There is only one rule
On this Wild Playground,
For every sign Hafiz has ever seen
Reads the same.
They all say,
'Have fun, my dear; my dear, have fun,
In the Beloved's Wonderful Game.'
—Hafiz (translated by Daniel Ladinsky)

Sometimes I have to stop and ask myself, can that possibly be true? Can the Universe's only rule really be "Have fun?" In all honesty, the idea that this is life's only requirement is actually a shockingly subversive statement for either 14th century Persia or today's world. It's certainly not something I ever heard from the nuns in Catholic school.

We've created so many rules for ourselves — from tax laws to relationship rituals, even nuances of e-mail etiquette — that it's hard to believe there could only be one rule that matters. Today alone, I've scrutinized three different parking signs just to make sure an honest mistake wouldn't cost me fifty bucks or result in having my car towed.

That's why a seemingly simplistic message like this one (or "Don't Worry, Be Happy!") is met with a lot of knee-jerk resistance.

If you tell someone who's complaining that "There's

only one rule in life: Have Fun," they will inevitably roll their eyes and tell you about their mortgage or their carpool. Our conditioned response is to defend (and define) ourselves as Responsible People, grownups who understand that life isn't just "fun and games."

And yet, in some areas of my life, I've grown less rule-bound. In fact, the more yoga classes I teach, the more relaxed I am about everyone following directions. These days, if I've instructed something that seems too challenging or the class just seems less than excited about a pose, I'll counter with, "Well, it was just a suggestion. My only rule is that you keep breathing."

I want to keep loosening up even more. I want to keep getting better at realizing the world won't end if _____ (you fill in the blank) doesn't happen.

Belle perfectly illustrates this easy-breezy worldview for me. She lives from a place of absolute knowing that there's nothing to be fixed and nothing we need to accomplish. According to my chocolate lab, we never need to prove our worthiness or justify our existence or redeem ourselves. Operating from the starting premise that "All is Well," her focus is entirely (and passionately!) on having fun.

THE POWER OF PUDDLES

My Aunt Gen once gave me an inspirational plaque that reminded me to stop and smell the roses.

Belle, on the other hand — rather than strolling through the proverbial rose garden — would much rather charge and splash through the muddiest puddles she can find.

Last year, Belle and I spent a fantastic rainy fall and

winter in Vancouver, and on our daily walks she managed to muddy herself no matter what. Even on those rare days when it wasn't raining, alongside every trail she managed to find some babbling brook or stream. Basically, she was powerless to resist any opportunity to cavort in the mud.

At first, this was really frustrating — our house had white carpets — but still, I had to admire that Belle simply wasn't afraid to get muddy. She'd found something that made her totally happy and she made no apologies for it.

Amazingly, this kind of muddy activity — or even just playing in the sand box — is something that many of us loved as kids, but have lost along the way. No longer bakers of mud pies, we have been compelled by adulthood to literally "clean up our acts" and are afraid to get our designer clothes or business suits dirty. Unlike Belle, we've forgotten that sometimes it's fun to get a little messy.

Although Belle doesn't know it, there's also a deep and important significance to mud in spiritual symbolism.

In the Eastern tradition, the lotus is often thought of as the most beautiful flower, and yet the irony is that it only grows up from the mud and muck. Countless teachers have talked about this as an analogy for everyone's spiritual path. Basically, we are rising up from the muck, aiming for the fresh air of freedom.

For all these reasons and more, I've always loved the Oscar Wilde quote **"We are all in the gutter, but some of us are looking at the stars."** That in a nutshell is the entire point of any spiritual practice.

We can't deny our muddy origins. In fact, we have to first accept where we are in the chaos and confusion of life, before achieving beautiful, transcendent peace of mind.

Making peace with where we are — accepting our mud and muck — is always the first step towards any lasting or meaningful change.

Of course, I'm not saying that this is what a puddle represents to Belle. For her, a puddle is less a reminder of our universal spiritual journey, than just another chance to have fun. Each puddle on the trail is just another offering from a bountiful universe that wants her to splash around and frolic as much as she possibly can.

Seeing her joy in cavorting in the mud, I can't resist smiling. Rising up from my own mental muck, I'm almost like a kid again, certain that fun is the name of the game.

A DOG'S LIFE

Many people — myself included — wish they had Belle's life. She sleeps as much as she wants. All her meals are provided for her. She enjoys days full of play-dates with dog pals Dwayne and Dingo, hikes in the canyons, and trips to the beach. And, like Angelina Jolie, she can't step outside the apartment without the world lavishing attention on her and being awed by her beauty.

You might think that Belle leads a charmed life of play mostly because she doesn't have to work. In actuality— and in Belle's mind—the opposite is true. She's working all the time.

In his bestseller *Cesar's Way*, Cesar Milan proclaims that every happy dog "needs a job," knowing that for canines the line between work and play is non-existent. Participating and engaging in life are all that matters.

One of Belle's many "jobs" is carrying *The New York Times* upstairs after our morning walk. So devoted is she

Living totally in the present means there's no split between work and play, or between jobs and games

to this Job/Game, that if someone swipes our paper, I must substitute something else so that she can have her full morning Work/Play experience.

And if Belle were ever to pen her resume, I'm sure she'd include Watch Dog on her list of avocations. Although she loves everyone lavishly, as though on patrol, she's alert to every nuance in her surrounding environment.

For Belle there's no split between work and play, or between jobs and games. Knowing that life is all about having fun, literally everything she does falls into the same category of Job/Game, Work/Play.

FLOW, Csíkszentmihályi's landmark book on "the psychology of optimal experience," explores this phenomenon and how it applies to us humans. He describes Flow in the same way I'd describe yoga: **"Being completely involved in an activity for its own sake. The ego falls away. Time flies. Every action, movement, and thought follows inevitably from the previous one, like playing jazz. Your whole being is involved, and you're using your skills to the utmost."**

I love that feeling and strive for it. I often feel it while I'm teaching a class where everyone — myself included —

gets lost in the Flow. I find it in music that carries me away, or the soaring narrative of a great film, book, or play.

I don't want to experience a constant contrast between Fun and Drudgery. Like Belle, I want my primary job to be enjoying life so much that there's pretty much no distinction between work and play, everything becoming part of the same joyful Flow.

LIGHTENING UP AND TUMBLING DOWN TO EARTH

Even though I've attended thousands of yoga classes, for me there's still always something a little wacky about watching a roomful of grownups struggling to balance on one leg in Tree Pose. Honestly, doesn't that seem as though it should be inherently goofy?

More than once while teaching a group class, I've wondered if I've really just graduated to playing Simon (or in my case "Edward") Says at an adult level. "Edward Says...Put your foot behind your head. Edward Says... keep it there and roll up to balance on your hands for *Chakorasana.*"

Belle's never impressed when I achieve a fancy new shape—one that would dazzle my students and even my fellow teachers. Sensitive as she is to my emotional states, she's just not that curious about my physical contortions. She could care less if I can balance in one-armed handstand or if I topple over.

The reality is that I'm coaxing people into all kinds of crazy shapes — things they probably would never have thought of on their own in a million years — in order to open up and free the energy in their bodies. As with the fable of the Emperor's new clothes, I wouldn't fault a sane person for wondering if standing on your head is really necessary for enlightenment. (I'll let you in on a little secret: Actually, it's not.)

In the same way, I've taught lots of private clients with dogs and no canine has ever taken the slightest notice when his or her master executes a breakthrough pose. At most, a dog will exhibit a generous attitude of "Well, if you really want to do that with your body, go ahead."

Belle's only real interest in my headstand practice is that it brings my face closer to the ground, making it more convenient for licking. It's been years since I've tumbled out of a standard inversion, but it's much trickier to balance upside down when someone's nuzzling your face. Assaulted by affection, I invariably collapse.

Substitute pretty much anything we do to impress ourselves or others — awards, job titles, corner offices, trophy wives, you name it — for "yoga poses" and you get the point. It's completely impossible to win Belle over with anything superficial. She's only interested in sharing her bottom-line of joy.

Of course there's nothing wrong with attempting complicated yoga poses or setting goals for any area of your life. What's important is to maintain a playful, Belle-like attitude about it all. Any activity that brings us joy is worth pursuing.

Every time I fall out of a shape, I try to remember that there's nothing more at stake here than my having fun — and that, coupled with Belle rushing in and licking my face, usually does put things back into proper, fun-loving, yogic perspective.

ALL FUN AND GAMES

At the very heart of yoga lies the concept of *Lila* (pronounced "Leela") which literally means "pastime, "sport," or as it's most commonly translated, "play."

For yogis, *Lila* defines our universe as the outcome of the creative play of the Divine (or God or Source or even Brahman—feel free to pick your own term). Simply stated, the Divine created the universe as a vast cosmic playground, and we're pretty much here for the fun of playing on it.

Why play? Surely there's got to be more of a point to our existence. It seems ridiculous to actually think that the vast universe is constructed as a cosmic game, a vast and eternal Disneyland where the Divine explores all possible experiences. Has the entire cosmos really been created just so Belle and I can toss a Frisbee on the beach?

We are so conditioned to think that either things are broken and we are here to fix them, or that we are broken ourselves and must be redeemed/saved/improved.

Lila, on the other hand, is never driven by goals or towards an outcome. *Lila* is what motivates Belle's splashing around in the pool for the sheer joy of it. Like Frisbee Fetch on the beach, it flies in the very face of our notion that we've got to get something accomplished and/or get some mess straightened out.

I lose touch with *Lila* all the time, lapsing into a work-oriented, "gotta fix things" mentality. My "To Do" list inflates to grandiose proportions, and I begin describing myself as a workaholic, almost as though I've won a merit badge.

When I go astray like this, I'm always looking for ways

to get back in synch. Perhaps the quickest cure I've discovered is to find someone who's fully connected to this energy — like Belle or a toddler — and watch them play.

I'd like to think I take Belle to the dog run out of some noble spirit of caretaking and responsible pet ownership, but many afternoons, I know I'm doing it just as much for myself. More than just stepping away from my laptop, enjoying Belle's unbridled exuberance lets me reconnect with my own suppressed reservoirs of enthusiasm.

It's ironic to think that I, the human — and allegedly the "master" in this relationship — literally feel chained to my desk whereas Belle can only and endlessly celebrate her freedom.

Of course, one glance at Belle having fun does not always produce "instant cosmic realignment." In fact, as is often the case, if I'm feeling particularly disconnected and she keeps dropping a toy into my lap while I'm trying to write — like right now, for example — I travel further from the connected spirit of play.

As I say, I'm lucky. Belle's constantly on call to teach me how one can indulge in *Lila*. If I don't resist, she's more than happy to remind me about the universe's one rule: HAVE FUN. Anytime I want — through the magic of play — Belle is willing to remind me of her second secret and demonstrate exactly how to frolic my way back to joy.

NEVER GIVE UP

How Belle gets pretty much everything she wants out of life through the power of persistence

Belle is a true master at getting what she wants — food, attention, exercise — but it isn't always instantly given to her. When she wants to play, she'll drop a toy repeatedly in my lap until I acquiesce and toss it for a few rounds. Or she'll sit patiently while I eat, hoping I'll choose to share a bite of food. If at first she doesn't succeed, she'll usually keep going until she does. On multiple levels, she demonstrates the power of persistence.

One of the key yoga sutras says that for the practice to work, for it to really bring us the peace of mind we're basically all after, it has to be consistent, enthusiastic, and done over a long period of time (1:14). Like Belle burying a bone, we've got to keep digging. There's always more to discover, always another layer to peel, and definitely more to let go of.

Yoga is strong medicine for our hearts, minds, and bodies, but it isn't a quick cure. Yes, many people feel terrific after just one yoga class, but this is a practice designed to open us up and heal us on many levels over extended periods of time. To the best of my knowledge, as good as they may be, no one has reached enlightenment after watching one Rodney Yee DVD.

The Dalai Lama was once asked how long a person should stay with a spiritual path to see if it was improving their lives. He replied, "I'd give it a little time....Maybe ten years."

Sometimes we can experience instantaneous and quantum breakthroughs, yet there really are no spiritual shortcuts or loopholes. You can gloss over things in your inner life that you need to address, but you will definitely be held back — if not completely controlled — by what you're ignoring.

For me, Belle's persistence in getting what she wants illustrates how I might apply myself with the same optimistic diligence. Ultimately, that kind of persistence — whether it's to be included in a car trip or progress in a spiritual path — always pays off.

TRAINING THE PUPPY

Meditation is very much like training a puppy. You put the puppy down and say, "Stay." Does the puppy listen? It gets up and it runs away. You sit the puppy back down again. "Stay." And the puppy runs away over and over again. Sometimes the puppy jumps up, runs over, and pees in the corner or makes some other mess. Our minds are much the same as the puppy, only they create even bigger messes. In training the mind, or the puppy, we have to start over and over again.
— Jack Kornfield, *A Path With Heart*

Nowhere is Belle's mastery of persistence better demonstrated than in her waiting for food.

She is, of course, perfectly well-fed — her vet recently confirmed that she is at her ideal weight — but like all labs, she loves to eat.

I confess to long ago breaking the cardinal rule that one shouldn't share "people food" with one's pet. Yet like countless other dog lovers, I am simply powerless to resist giving Belle something that so easily brings her such pleasure. Frankly, it feels cruel and sadistic not to offer her a scrap of whatever I'm enjoying.

Belle, however, has learned that she can't overtly beg or she will definitely NOT be rewarded. Some restraint is necessary. Jumping into someone's lap will not result in her getting the treat she's craving.

Instead, she has mastered the art of sitting and waiting patiently, refusing to budge (or even break eye contact) until she's obtained her reward or the meal is consumed.

For me, it's a perfect model for meditation. Frankly, her sitting there silently even looks like my meditation practice, except that she is much better than I am at both concentrating and not fidgeting.

I love the mind/puppy meditation analogy because it acknowledges just how restless our minds are and at the same time encourages us to be gentle in our approach to disciplining our thoughts. We all know how it feels to have a rampage of ideas scampering around our brains. Just as we must train the puppy by constant practice and repetition, so we have to be disciplined yet compassionate towards ourselves as we approach a meditation practice.

Knowing that every well-trained, perfectly-behaved dog started out as a rambunctious pup can give us hope that however unruly our minds are, we might just gain some ground in our quest for serenity. Through the practice of meditation, our minds can be transformed from unruly rascals to loving friends. The only secret is that it takes a little time and a lot of persistence.

THE ARTFUL NUDGE

Belle will bump her head just underneath my forearm or my elbow. It's very gentle — barely a tap — but it's impossible to ignore. In fact, it makes typing or eating difficult. And she'll usually do it over and over until I acquiesce.

At first, Belle's persistent nudging annoys me, but then always makes me laugh. It sometimes happens when there's food involved and sometimes just when she wants attention.

Being interrupted and taken out of your flow is of course always a little irritating. However, it's basically very sweet, and she's always smiling when she does it. Belle's artful nudge is a little reminder — "I'm here!" or "Let's share that food!" Or sometimes just a way of checking in and asking "How are you?"

If, as Woody Allen said, **"Eighty percent of success is showing up,"** then the other twenty percent has got to be "following up." Belle's taught me that not only is the occasional nudge effective and necessary, it really is an art. Even though things flow pretty smoothly for me most of the time, we live in a busy world where this form of persistence is valuable.

Today I got a check that someone had promised to send six weeks ago — someone who has totally great intentions and is completely trustworthy — but if I hadn't sent a reminder email, he might have forgotten for months.

The same is true for our spiritual practices. It's important that we be both consistent in whatever we've chosen, but also that we are willing to keep things fresh and alive. Like cross-training for the soul, sometimes you have to shake things up a bit to really move forward. Every now and then you have to give yourself a spiritual nudge.

I'm always a little shocked when I meet a yoga teacher who's unwilling to try a different style of class. Some types of yoga classes are so different from each other, you might not even think they were branches from the same spiritual tree. As passionate as I am about the flowing movement style I've been trained in, I definitely sometimes feel the need for a completely different yoga experience. It always expands me and enhances my own teaching.

Getting locked into only one tradition in anything can result in stagnation, or worse, fundamentalism. Just like Belle nudging me, sometimes I need to read teachings from the Bible or the Sufis or Kabbalah to progress spiritually. Belle's taught me that while part of persistence is staying the course, sometimes a willingness to explore another perspective offers an artful and spiritual nudge that lets me reach my goal. Alongside waiting patiently for the miracle to happen, sometimes you've just got to nudge it along.

BIG DOG MENTALITY

In yoga, the greatest use of persistence would be to achieve and sustain a lasting state of peace of mind, or what I like to call a Big Dog Mentality.

I admit to having a prejudice towards big dogs (and one big dog in particular) yet in my travels I have definitely met my share of smaller dogs whom I have admired and adored. Growing up we had a dachshund who was supremely sweet and two of my closest friends now have toy breeds with whom Belle has instantly bonded.

More important than any canine's actual physical size is his or her attitude. Even the tiniest chihuahua can embody the spirit of a Great Dane. (And frankly, having no sense of her poundage, during a cross-country drive, Belle spent most of the time curled up in my friend Jude's lap!)

One of the endlessly amusing things about walking a dog of a larger breed is that the loudest barks we encounter on our strolls are inevitably from the smallest dogs. It's just plain funny when a five-pound chihuahua barks her head off at my 80 pound labrador. Meanwhile, Belle always has a completely serene non-reaction to all the yipping and yapping. It just doesn't ruffle her feathers (or her fur) in the least.

Although in some ways I like the gutsiness of the little dogs making their Napoleonic statements when they encounter Belle, I prefer Belle's stately dignity. She's the proverbial Big Dog in the situation, never losing her cool or composure despite the attempts of others to create chaos around her.

The yoga sutras define yoga as **"calming the storms of the mind."** (1:2) There's an old proverb about not being able to rile the Buddha even if you drove an oxcart over him. That's perhaps the ultimate embodiment of the Big Dog Mentality, knowing that no matter what life hurtles at you, your serenity is unshakeable.

Although I admire that kind of equipoise, it's no surprise I am eons from achieving it. I am, however, constantly getting better at letting things go, not sweating the proverbial small stuff, and trying to draw from my meditation practice in gnarly situations.

More and more, I find myself able to allow the people, things, and even thoughts that are yipping at my heels to coexist with me, without distressing me. Like Belle, I want to be able to simply stroll along on my own path, effortlessly living the Big Dog Mentality of increasingly unshakeable serenity.

SECRET #4
EVERYONE IS YOUR FRIEND
Belle's self-fulfilling prophecy regarding friendship

During the course of any given day, several dozen times I will move from one room to the next, only to find that Belle's repositioned herself and lain her head on my feet while I'm washing the dishes or unjamming the laser printer. My changing locations just gives her an additional opportunity to show me one more time how much she loves me.

I have a military-minded, stealth-fighter pilot friend who describes Belle as "a love machine." He jokingly compares her to the Terminator, except that she's on a continuous, unstoppable mission to share her overflowing affection not just with me but with everyone she encounters.

We humans live like there's a chronic shortage of love, as though it's something we must ration. People are always searching for the perfect person and the perfect moment to let themselves feel love. Not so with dogs. They have no trouble instantly tuning into love's abundant possibilities.

Master yoga teacher Erich Schiffman promises that yoga can help us achieve a similar mindset. Through a committed yoga practice, **"all the world will take on a friendly and nonthreatening glow"** — exactly Belle's take on all her relationships.

People are twice as likely to speak to a person with a dog than without one and when they do speak, people feel more comfortable much more quickly. That's why guys often describe dogs as "chick magnets" — so many barriers of approachability instantly dissolve just by having a canine at your side.

When I'm by myself running errands, I can cruise along swiftly, saying thanks when my credit card gets swiped and handed back to me and heading on my efficient, solitary way. Walking around with Belle, however, always results in a dozen spontaneous encounters with strangers, moments where people pay her compliments or even stop me to ask if their toddler can say "hello" and pet my dog.

On any given day, almost every dog owner can recall his or her pet showing them affection, but how many of us can, each day, think of another person doing the same?

If you simply believe that people exist for you to love them and for them to love you back, then — while there may be a few exceptions you'll need to shrug off — overwhelmingly this will become more and more true for you. Believing that people are inherently there to connect with her and make friends, not only enriches Belle's own life, but also completely transforms mine. Belle's friendliness becomes a self-fulfilling prophecy of the best possible kind.

THINK THE BEST OF EVERYONE

"If I accept you as you are, I will make you worse; however if I treat you as though you are what you are capable of becoming, I help you become that."
—Goethe

One early morning I was walking Belle and returning to my building. The streets were still relatively deserted, with storefront grates down and bolted shut.

A relatively non-descript, middle-aged man was walking along the street. We were probably a good twenty feet away when somehow we startled him. Almost as though Belle were an unchained rabid wolf about to violently attack him, he flung himself against the metal grate.

Chocolate labs as a breed, and Belle in particular, are perhaps the least scary dog in the world. I'd trust Belle to guard a baby in a cradle (but maybe not a roast beef sandwich). Having watched her unfazed as toddlers pull her tail and poke her, I can't imagine her ever getting angry at anyone.

The poor guy who flung himself into the metal grate, terrified of the "scary" big dog, was completely creating that reality in his own mind. I'm sure it felt necessary and realistic — strategic even — to react that way but none of it was empirically true. Belle was smiling, her tail was wagging, and frankly, she wasn't even noticing him. Whatever his ongoing story about dogs was, it was so powerful that he had projected her right into it and created a reality where a vicious dog was attacking him.

We forget how powerful our stories about relationships can be towards shaping our reality. I've heard many women say "There are just no single guys in New York City," when in fact, according to the US Census, there are literally well over a million. Not surprisingly, most of my happily married friends just didn't sing that tune.

One of the best yoga practices for reshaping our stories about our relationships is *Metta* or Loving-Kindness Meditation, where one methodically generates positive feelings towards others.

Metta Meditation always begins with first sending love towards oneself, then working one's way through the Benefactor (someone one feels entirely positive about), the Friend, the Neutral Party, and finally the Enemy (someone one feels largely negative about). Ultimately, the goal is a state of mind where everyone, even one's enemy is viewed as equally worthy of compassion. All our artificial barriers dissolve until only a universal feeling of love exists.

Belle doesn't need this practice. Like Will Rogers, she's never met a man she hasn't liked. Life hasn't taught her that people are dangerous or difficult or out to screw her over. Instead, it's pretty much the case that people either adore her, or the ones who "just aren't that into dogs," simply dissolve into the background.

Years ago I went through a streak of difficult landlord relationships. I saw landlords, more or less, as one tiny step above ravenous wolves, albeit wolves armed with lawyers. It all felt very, very true — and I could convince anyone of my story — but I realized that these beliefs were self-perpetuating.

It was far from instantaneous, but with some *Metta* meditation I began to re-humanize these people in my mind. Amazingly, once I truly generated a feeling of compassion and empathy, everything shifted. I witnessed an unfortunate occurrence that affected one of the landlords — the accidental destruction of an important piece of the property — and my heart went out to my former enemy. I'm not talking about a big hugging moment, or even clearing the air over a round of drinks, but somehow we had subtly reestablished a connection as people. From that point onwards, our dealings were always more pleasant. Sometimes just by thinking the best of someone rather than the worst, things change.

I'm not saying that with *Metta* meditation difficult people are instantly transformed into saints. Rather, by shifting my own viewpoint, I no longer found myself continually flinging myself against those grates and defending myself against attacks, real or imaginary. Instead, like Belle, I can simply let folks pass on their way, silently blessing them as they drift out of my life, no longer part of any drama, but still part of a universal, loving flow.

BEING A SOCIAL ANIMAL

I once had a gallery show of my visual art that was within walking distance from my home on the Lower East Side of New York City. Belle was always welcome at the gallery and so she was completely thrilled by the opening night party populated by all my friends (who were of course, merely a subset of Belle's friends). When it was time for Belle to be taken home and for me to join some buyers and friends for a post-opening drink, Belle simply wouldn't leave. My sweet little dog dug her heels into the ground and wouldn't budge.

It's extraordinarily rare that Belle is that willful and disobedient. Some would find her behavior a little, well, bratty, but I appreciated her persistence and her logic. Her values were so clearly communicated — I want to be with my friends — that she must have thought there was some huge mistake being made. Almost as though we were canceling Christmas, she simply couldn't comprehend why she should be required to leave a gathering filled with all the people she loved. Ultimately, I had to take her halfway home myself before she accepted the fact that for her the party was indeed over.

Sangha is a Sanskrit word meaning "community." While there are all sorts of spiritual traditions and practices in both the East and the West that involve solitude and isolation, it's far more prevalent that one's journey takes place alongside others of like-mindedness. Like canines, we are fundamentally social animals. We don't have to

We are traveling our spiritual paths with other people.

join a monastery or a nunnery, but we are traveling our spiritual paths with other people.

Dogs are keenly aware of the power of community, of sangha. Canine behaviorists tell us that dogs always define themselves as part of a pack. Even if we think we're just a bunch of dysfunctional strangers who happen to be genetically related or sharing a large apartment we all found on Craig's List, we always form some kind of tribe.

At their best, the people you hang out with regularly can completely elevate your life, support you, and encourage you to greatness. On the other hand, they can become the proverbial bad influences that might not ruin your life, but could keep you stuck, stagnant, and bitter.

Sangha might be as traditional as finding a yoga center where you love the classes, teachers, and fellow students. It might even be artistic, such as a group of directors and actors who enjoy collaborating with each other so much that they create film after film, or play after play.

It's entirely up to you how you utilize your community for your best growth. For a wise lover of mankind like Belle, *sangha* can become a major pathway towards happiness and an awesome life.

Often one of the false premises of friendship is that friends must always agree on things. If I hate someone, so should you. If I'm depressed, you should support my worldview that life is indeed difficult and painful.

Belle, on the other hand, does not believe in these rules. However much she loves me, Belle will never stoop to my level. Instead, she'll invite me to climb towards hers. She firmly maintains her own higher emotional ground, letting me know I have an open invitation to meet her there.

As Swami Satchidananda says in his commentary on the Sutras **"A liberated person can come into the world and be useful to it but is not affected by it."** It is as though spiritual development gives us "nice thick rubber gloves which allow us to touch any voltage without damage."

Belle will lick my face but will not bite the person who has annoyed me. She will not join me in worry about the American Express bill but she will rest her head in my lap and stare lovingly at me. She will not toss and turn over my romantic tribulations, but she will always cuddle beside me in bed.

The truest of friends, she will only love me and remind me that at every moment, ultimately all is well. Although this lacks the short-term satisfaction of gaining lots of agreement from my trying-to-be-supportive human friends, I believe this is actually far more helpful.

By not descending to my depressed or frustrated state, she always offers me the benefits of her own, far greater spiritual alignment. I can choose to remain miserable, or rise up to her present-moment, fun-based philosophy of well-being. More and more with my own human friends, I try to offer the same possibility.

LOYALTY

Loyalty is about the security that comes when you know you can trust those you love. Applied to Belle, it means that I can allow her the freedom of being off leash.

The first few times I took Belle hiking, I worried about letting her run free. During her puppyhood in Connecticut, there was an electric fence to ensure she stayed on the property, and in New York City I always obey the leash laws. I've never for a second doubted Belle's love for me, but I wondered if a momentary distraction like a fleeting deer or just the opportunity to run unbounded might lead her astray.

One bucolic day in Runyon Canyon, I decided to trust her loyalty and take the risk. Amazingly, Belle either stayed right by my side, or else she pranced a little ahead before turning back to make sure that I was following her! It was clear that she'd fully embraced the idea of us as an unbreakable team.

Dogs like Belle define loyalty. As pack animals, they live their lives through community and family. The Native Americans of the Southwest and Plains all had dogs who warned of approaching danger, helped in the hunt, or watched over their families. Incorporated into a household, all breeds of dogs demonstrate pride at pleasing their owners and satisfaction from their belonging to a clan.

A dog's loyalty is particularly wonderful in that it blends the gentle sweetness of a best friend with a fierce, protective feeling. I know that Belle would never hurt me, but on a primal level I also know that she would do anything to protect the ones she loves.

In a world of broken vows, Belle adores me "for richer or poorer, in sickness and in health" no matter what.

> A dog's loyalty is particularly wonderful in that it blends the gentle sweetness of a best friend with a fierce, protective feeling.

Certainly, unlike many humans, dogs are never looking to "trade up" in their personal relationships. No dog ever left someone for a bigger yard or better food, much less for something as ridiculous as money or fame. No dog ever decided to "shop around and try out a bunch of owners before settling down with one." While Belle loves everyone, I am eternally appreciative that I am indeed her very best friend.

UNCONDITIONAL LOVE

One morning I took Belle on a particularly long walk, as a means, frankly, of distracting myself from dreary personal problems I was stewing over. Preoccupied, I suddenly realized that she was being lavishly complimented by the movie star Liv Tyler, the magical elf Arwen of *The Lord of The Rings*. Belle and I chatted with Liv and her King Charles Spaniel for about fifteen minutes before heading home.

Ten minutes later, we ran into Jamal, a homeless man on the Lower East Side who adores Belle. In fact, a few

Living with a loyal dog helps anyone feel more secure about life.

months before in the winter, he told me he was "living for the summer just to see Belle play in the sprinklers in the park with the kids again."

Most people, myself included, tend to be much more interested in hanging out with beautiful movie stars than snaggletoothed homeless men. Not Belle, however. As though looking through the eyes of a great saint, Belle sees no difference between them, lavishing her affection equally on Jamal and Liv Tyler. Unlike myself, she's "starstruck" by all of humanity.

Belle's spirit of boundless inclusion inspires less spiritually-advanced beings like myself. A tremendous amount of letting go on my part would be necessary to approach her level of unconditional love. She allows everyone to be exactly who they are without comparing or condemning anyone. This absence of judgment creates a joyful, connecting energy that is incredibly expansive.

Sharon Salzberg writes that **"A mind filled with love can be likened to the sky with a variety of clouds moving through it — some light and fluffy, others ominous and threatening. No matter what the situation, the sky is not affected by the clouds. It is free."** Through yoga practice, **"We develop, as the Buddha advised to do, a power of love, compassion, joy and equanimity so strong that our mind becomes like space that cannot be painted, or like the pure river that cannot be burned."**

Belle exemplifies this boundless energy of cosmic connection because she allows everyone and everything.

Completely in touch with her own inherent worthiness, she's able to view everyone else in the same way. She allows everyone else to be exactly who they are and appreciates them no matter what. The vastness of her compassion gives Belle a proverbial heart as wide as the world.

Living with a loyal dog helps anyone feel more secure about life.

EXPRESS YOURSELF

How Belle communicates so powerfully with the world

ASK FOR WHAT YOU REALLY WANT

The breeze at dawn has secrets to tell you.
Don't go back to sleep.

You must ask for what you really want.
Don't go back to sleep.
— Rumi (translated by Coleman Barks)

Belle has absolutely no problem asking for what she wants.

Even without words, no matter what the situation, there's absolutely no doubt about what she's asking for whenever she fixes those amber eyes on you.

We humans, however, are far less straightforward. In fact, we often downplay or even deny what we truly desire most.

We don't ask for the raise we know we deserve. We stay stuck in bad relationships, or else we never let that special someone know how we really feel.

Why is it the case that we, gifted with speech and strategy, can't express our desires, whereas Belle never holds back? How is it that our fear of rejection somehow trumps the possibility of our greater happiness? Why is the "no" so dreaded that we don't even risk asking the question?

Belle takes none of my "no's" personally. Simply put, she's in touch with her inherent worthiness, while we are not. Her self-esteem is not contingent on my sharing my lunch with her. If denied, she may lobby for another round of Fetch but pretty quickly she moves forward with her life.

We humans, on the other hand, are not nearly as solidly

We often downplay or even deny what we truly desire most.

secure in who we are. We take any and all rejection painfully to heart, assuming we've got to adjust or fix something about ourselves to win some universal, never-ending popularity contest.

Yoga teaches us that we are not only completely worthy, our true nature is divine. The ultimate goal of the practice is *samadhi*, **"a state in which the aspirant is one with the object of his meditation, the Supreme Spirit pervading the universe, where there is a feeling of unutterable joy and peace."** (Iyengar's *Light on Yoga*) What yoga teaches us is how to remove all the barriers to that truth, to our complete, intrinsic worthiness.

Unlike Belle, who was born knowing she was worthy and has never forgotten this, as adults we have to relearn this truth. If we follow her example and more and more freely EXPRESS OURSELVES, we'll learn that now is always the time to boldly ask for what we really want.

USE YOUR WORDS (WELL)

"Use your words" is a phrase that I hear my friends who are parents employ all the time, but it was never part of my own growing up. (Sometimes — as a joke — I'll say it to Belle when she's staring at me expectantly, often attracting the curious looks of passersby.)

One of the key things I've learned from training Belle is the power of language when it's specific and targeted.

I try not to send mixed messages or weak ones to Belle, or to anyone else.

For example, I grew up in a house where we would shout "Come" ten or twenty times before my untrained childhood dog chose to obey. In obedience classes with Belle, I've learned that you must train a dog to respond to the first and only repetition of a command, never issuing one if you aren't able to enforce it.

Knowing this, at first, I taught "Come" to Belle at a short distance while she was on a leash. Then I began incorporating food rewards which always sent her running. Now with treats only given some of the time, she's learned to follow the command perfectly. (If she doesn't quickly comply, I have another trick — I simply move in the opposite direction and she immediately charges towards me; please note, this also works amazingly well in most romantic relationships.)

My childhood dogs, however, were given such unclear messages it's no wonder they did what we wanted only 50% of the time and only when it suited them. They were good dogs at heart, but we'd failed to have any power behind our language other than expressing our own frustration when it wasn't working.

When my friend Jude opened her yoga center, she wanted the right Sanskrit word to convey this concept of setting an intention, of being determined but not forced. *Sankalpah* is the name she chose for her studio because it means living and practicing from that place of having a clear focus. When *sankalpah* is applied to language, the commands I use with my dog have real power, not so much to make her bend to my will, but to allow us to communicate.

More than just "sit," "stay," and "come," canine behaviorists tell us that the average trained dog can understand 160 different words. While almost all of us dog owners are deeply underestimating the potential of language to connect with our dog, we often ignore the power of words in our own lives.

Beyond the obvious ways in which we can hurt each other with malicious language, more subtle ways abound. Making unfulfilled promises, for example, is parallel to repeating a command to a puppy you're not able to enforce. In both cases, the words mean nothing.

Truthfully, it is the intention behind the words that makes something uplifting or damaging, but often an undercurrent of subliminal meaning seems small but can be really significant. Lately I've been examining my own use of humor, particularly sarcasm. (The root of sarcasm, incidentally, is from the Greek *sarkazein* meaning "to tear flesh.") Simply by modifying a few sarcastic jokes I've tended to make about myself in banter, I've seen powerful changes in my life.

Obviously calling something a "challenge" rather than a "problem" might not instantly improve a situation, but nonetheless it helps build a more helpful mental framework. Ultimately committing to a spirit of sankalpah behind every word we speak or write over the long term might just have enormous transformative power. As puppy obedience school taught me, this kind of awareness means the difference between a wandering pup and a dog who runs faithfully into your arms each and every time you call her.

A PERFECT TIME TO DOG PADDLE

In Runyon Canyon there are three main water stations, each with a faucet and a water bowl. Belle, however, invariably choses not to drink from the water bowl (she

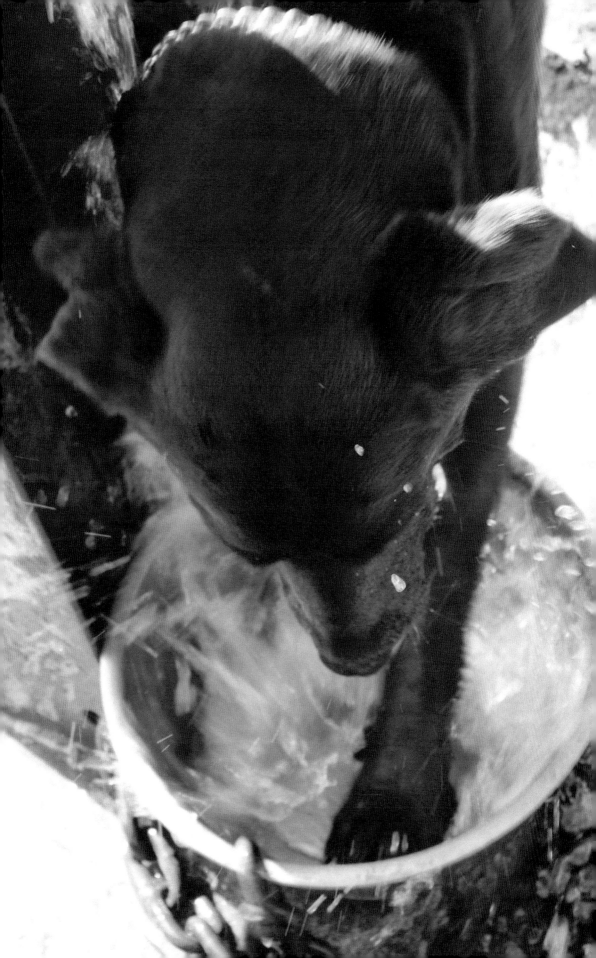

prefers me to turn on the faucet and then she enjoys the water drinking-fountain style). Instead, as a natural born swimmer, every time there's any body of water available (no matter the size, puddle or Pacific) she has to dive in. She'll furiously start paddling in the water dish until every drop has been splashed away. If I refill it for the next dog, she'll repeat this if she can. Her love of swimming is so deeply ingrained that even three inches of water means she's got to attempt a dip.

Passersby always laugh when they see my 80-pound dog trying to swim in the equivalent of a medium-sized salad bowl. I love that she's just going for it: she's simply got to express her love of the water and if the medium isn't big enough to hold her dreams, so be it.

So many of us are waiting for the perfect set of conditions before we make our move. We want an assurance, the proverbial engraved invitation, that everything is completely lined up before we act. At its worst, we can lead our lives dipping our toes into the water, never feeling that it's the ideal temperature to jump in and splash around.

I was once contemplating a major life decision and consulting with a mentor. I concluded with, "Now might not be the perfect time for..." and he cut me off. "There is no perfect time. There's no perfect time to quit your job or fall in love or have a baby. Anyone who tells you otherwise is kidding themselves."

And he was right, of course. Obviously, you don't dive headfirst into a three-foot pool, but what Belle has taught me is that if you want to swim, you've got to find a way to get wet.

Yogi Bhajan, the first guru to teach Kundalini to the West, had a personal motto: **"It's not the life that** matters, it's the courage that you bring to it." He offered five sutras for the Aquarian Age (aka the modern world). The first two are about interacting with others: "Understand through compassion; otherwise you might misunderstand the times" and "Recognize that the other person is you." The last three, however occur to me every time I see Belle transform a water bowl into an ocean:

When the time is on you, start and the pressure will be off.

There is a way through every block.

Vibrate the cosmos; the cosmos shall clear the path.

Or, as Goethe said, **"Whatever you can do or dream you can, begin it. Boldness has genius, power and magic in it!"**

I know this from experience. Recently, once I firmly made the decision to move across country, all sorts of things fell into place. An old friend resurfaced after five years, offering a perfect housing solution. The timing for everything began to flow better than I could have expected.

Like Belle, rather than waiting for the ocean to come to me, once I made a firm decision and expressed it — in other words, I started dog-paddling — the universe rewarded me with almost magical outcomes.

POWER OF ENTHUSIASM

"In times of joy, all of us wished we possessed a tail we could wag."
— Auden

My first major yoga teacher, Dana Flynn, won me over primarily with her intense enthusiasm for the practice.

She was madly, passionately in love with yoga and that sincerity was palpable. It made you stop and say — as the elderly lady did in the diner scene in *When Harry Met Sally* — "I'll have what she's having." No further selling was necessary.

Belle's enthusiasm for the things she loves most — primarily food, friends, and fun (the three "F's" of her universe) — manifests through her entire body. She literally vibrates with delight when she's presented with something or someone that pleases her.

When we play Fetch, right before each toss, barely able to contain herself, she prances up and down expectantly. So much enthusiasm is racing through her, she literally has to jump for joy. Often, I'm more than ready to quit after a few rounds but her boundless energy pretty much requires me to keep the game going.

As humans, however, more often than not we've been trained to play our cards close to the vest. We know we have to measure our words when meeting strangers, making sure our remarks and actions are appropriate. Nowhere is this more clear than in the elaborate courtship rituals of dating. Professional consultants can now be hired to make sure you look interested but not too eager, attracted but not desperate. We're convinced we need to mask our enthusiasm behind layers of cool or the other person will immediately run away, terrified that we might actually like them.

I once audited an acting workshop where everyone was captured on tape. In the interview portion of the exercise, overwhelmingly people who thought they were revealing their passions were underplaying and holding back. Whether they were striving for a veneer of professionalism, or simply trying to not look desperate and just "play it cool," one after another they masked

whatever enthusiasm they might have had. Whenever a rare individual was able to simply reflect his or her passion, however, the spark in his eyes or lilt of her voice was obvious and enormously appealing.

I love the origins of the word "enthusiasm." It's from the Greek word "*enthous*," literally meaning "inspired or possessed by a god." Rather than an embarrassment, our passions actually elevate and connect us to the Divine. We are at our most Cosmically Connected when we are completely wrapped up in our authentic enthusiasm.

We dog owners will testify that one of the most satisfying moments in our day is returning home to our dog's ebullient greeting. Every homecoming feels like Odysseus returning from decades lost at sea. On a daily basis, to your dog, you are a conquering hero, and that level of enthusiasm just makes us feel great about life.

Authentic enthusiasm has tremendous power. Remember, as the Yoga Sutras tell us, **"Practice becomes firmly grounded when well attended to for a long time, continuously, and with great enthusiasm."** (1:15)

It's not just enough to half-heartedly approach yoga or any spiritual system, or frankly anything you're devoting any significant time towards. You must do whatever it is you're doing with tremendous enthusiasm or else nothing major is going to happen.

As its ancient Greek root reveals, far beyond just lip-service or mindless cheerleading, enthusiasm is a powerful way to plug yourself directly into divine energy. That's the electricity, the cosmic voltage that can magically transform your world.

Without language, Belle's wagging tail reveals exactly what she's feeling.

Sometimes, when she's half-asleep, I'll play a little teasing game of reaching out to touch her and her tail will thump. Then I'll withdraw my hand, only to re-approach her and watch her tail thwack again. That tail is a total and sincere barometer of her love.

Belle is exactly who she is and is completely consistent in showing that to people. She's simply not capable of pretending otherwise. We humans, however, have tremendous capacity to deceive.

Satya is the Sanskrit word for truth, something yogis consider a vital part of their code of conduct. Beyond just not-lying, the more subtle meaning of satya incorporates the principle of non-violence (*ahimsa*). In other words, it not enough just to be blatantly honest, one must also use the truth for the welfare of others.

These concepts extend far beyond just the words we speak to our actions. One way of being untruthful and also harmful might be to aggressively attempt a physical yoga practice or any workout that's beyond one's limits. Not listening to the signals from your own body, denying their truth and forcing yourself into a shape, would violate both *satya* and *ahimsa* — and might require a visit to a chiropractor.

There are so many ways in which one might lead an untruthful life. One may fail to be honest about one's real feelings in relationships or towards one's career, and one may be motivated by reasons ranging from a misguided kindness to a cowardly convenience. All of us need to figure out the way in which we can be simultaneously honest and non-hurtful, even towards ourselves.

The absolute honesty of a loving animal like Belle offers an inspiring example. It's incredibly refreshing to see unrepressed emotions occurring spontaneously and delivered honestly, all against the background of her inherent kindness. That's the exact right blend of *satya* and *ahimsa*, one I want to model in all my interactions with others.

JUST DO IT

"It's much easier to apologize than it is to get permission."
— Rear Admiral Grace Hopper

Last summer, I arrived with Belle to visit my friend Genevieve's family on Shelter Island. After I opened the door to the rental car, like the people-loving animal she is, Belle happily greeted each person in the family, with particularly enthusiastic licking of the two squealing toddlers. Then, spying their swimming pool, Belle made an immediate beeline for the water. Not asking permission, but climbing right over and pretty much toppling the mesh-fence, Belle jumped into the pool and began swimming joyously. I can't imagine that any living creature has ever been happier than Belle was splashing around that August day. (Fortunately my friend Genevieve was highly amused, telling me, "Honestly, I wish all my guests would just say 'hello' and then dive into the pool. It would make being a weekend hostess so much simpler.")

I sometimes joke that Belle is a wicked dog, knowing of course that she's not. In her early days, it's true that once or twice, I'd leave a cheeseburger on the kitchen counter

and turning my back for a few moments to deal with a phone call, find that it had vanished.

She has learned, of course, that stealing food from the counter is forbidden yet, as with Genevieve's pool, she's still willing to test other limits. I admire that Belle's willing to take risks in pursuing what she really wants.

So much of my own life has been about hesitating, wondering if I'm going to step on anyone's toes or offend someone. As bold as many of my choices may have been, I've still held myself back more often than not by wondering "What will people think?" or "Will this ruffle some feathers?" More and more, I'm following Belle's lead, jumping in and figuring out later how to handle the consequences.

For many years I taught a fantastic New Year's Eve yoga class that ended at the stroke of midnight. Part of the ritual I created involved a fire ceremony I made up. My friend Dan showed me how magicians use something called flash paper. It's so highly flammable that it pretty much evaporates instantly, creating a bright flash of light. It dissolves so rapidly when ignited that you can even hold it in your hand and not get burned.

I wanted to open the New Year's Eve class with students writing the things they wanted to let go of on pieces of flash paper and then lighting them one by one over a central candle. The room would be dark except for everyone huddled around that candle, punctuated by bright flashes as each person let go of one burden after another.

I thought of asking the yoga center if this would be OK, but I took a lesson from Belle. I knew it would be completely safe — I'd researched and experimented with the flash paper myself — but I could understand that any business owner might get a little spooked if I started talking about conducting a mysterious midnight fire ceremony. I decided I would just do it, and if I got into trouble, I'd apologize after the fact.

The night was a fantastic success, with my fire ceremony being the absolute highlight. I'm sure word probably trickled back to the owners — I've never brought it up — but as a "done deed" without casualties or incident, there was no problem. Even now, my successors are still using it as part of the magic of that annual celebration.

Like Belle savoring my "abandoned" cheeseburger, I learned that when your heart's set on something it's better to just express yourself than trying to manage everyone's reaction or get unanimous approval.

In a world of committees, permission slips, waivers, and release forms, of course this isn't always possible. But rather than letting the approval of others dominate my life — and truthfully you can never consistently guarantee or manage other people's reactions anyway — I'm mastering EXPRESSING MYSELF and just going for what I want.

When it comes to my more heartfelt yet controversial decisions, I'm willing to take the risks, climb over the fence, and plunge into the swimming pool.

STAY CURIOUS

How Belle transforms every experience into something new, fresh, and interesting

EVERY RIDE IS A JOYRIDE

Dogs are among the most curious of animals. Puppies, in particular, are notorious for exploring everything and anything that comes along their path. Indeed, every time the doorbell rings, Belle's incredibly eager to see who might be coming up the stairs.

And every time I bring any bag whatsoever into the house, Belle must see what's inside. Far beyond hunger, she's just curious about what's inside the bag. Whenever I start feeling jaded, her unbelievable eagerness for experience is truly a breath of fresh air.

The Sufi-inspired modern philosopher A.H. Almaas writes extensively on the strong connection between curiosity and joy. **"You are free every moment that you are completely curious. You're completely in love, and who are you in love with? Who knows? You're just in love."**

It is curiosity that motivates the entire path of self-discovery that is yoga. Desikachar, a master teacher of great lineage, writes in *The Heart of Yoga* that **"Yoga is not an external experience. In yoga we try in every action to be as attentive as possible to everything we do. We observe what we are doing and how we are doing it. We do it only for ourselves. We are both observer and what is observed at the same time. If we do not pay attention to ourselves in our practice, then we cannot call it yoga."** In other words, to be a real yogi — or to follow any spiritual path — is to get very curious about yourself.

There are numerous styles of yoga but they have all this quality of observation in common. Although the poses free the energy of the body and support physical vitality, they are incidental, functioning first and foremost as tools for awareness. There's no claim that the physical shapes were delivered by Divine Powers to man. Rather

Belle constantly reminds me of not only the connection between curiosity and joy, but also that so many ordinary things deserve our full attention.

the sages were so consumed with curiosity they were literally willing to stand on their heads or bend into pretzels to see what they could learn about themselves.

Belle constantly reminds me of not only the connection between curiosity and joy, but also the truth that so many ordinary things deserve our full attention. Just as it's not necessary to do extreme shapes to successfully experience yoga, one's curiosity does not have to be focused on the obscure or exotic. An unpacked Whole Foods Bag on the kitchen floor, a gnarly old tennis ball, or a plastic water bottle she can carry up the stairs intrigue and inspire Belle completely.

In the same way, I've never been bored in a great beginner's yoga class. There's always something new, something fresh to explore. It's never old hat. As the saying goes, only the boring get bored.

That's why the most advanced yoga practices are not about achieving flamboyant shapes. Rather, the most seasoned yogis spend time intently watching the breath and observing the mind stilled in meditation.

In the end, if you're truly curious like Belle, the simplest things guide you on the path of curiosity and self-discovery, a path that simultaneously creates instant joy.

COLORING OUTSIDE THE LINES

Vets tell us that play is something dogs never outgrow, but it seems we only allow children to play until we can discipline it out of them. Somehow we're brainwashed into thinking that play and adulthood just don't go together.

Belle has a new friend, Dingo, a spunky stray mutt adopted by my neighbor during a drive through Texas. When Dingo and Belle see each other, tails wag wildly as their front paws rear up, and they meet in mid-air for a frozen, *Matrix*-like moment of gladiatorial combat.

My other neighbors have an equally scrappy dog named Dwayne, and he and Belle have their own games — usually chasing each other, followed by a tug of war on whatever empty plastic bottle they find in the park. From a distance these playfights and chases could look threatening, but they are always completely harmless, since Belle, Dingo, and Dwayne share the canine code for play.

When Belle meets a new dog, she makes a universally-understood gesture — a play bow, as it were — where she goes down to her elbows with her rear-end lifted and her tail wagging. Her mouth is open and her ears are pricked up. She just needs to do this for two or three seconds and it is clear to Dingo or Dwayne or any other dog that whatever happens next isn't "real." Most of us, however,

Playtime is always just a breath or two away.

are nowhere nearly as skilled at slipping into Playtime Mode.

For several years I taught one of the most advanced yoga classes in New York City, called "Cosmic Play." What made "Cosmic Play" so unique was that having taught something quite specific and given several challenging variations, I would then more or less encourage students to "play" with the ideas I offered on their own in whatever shapes they wished — a "freestyle" section of the class, as it were.

Interestingly, these moments of freedom were perhaps the most advanced aspect of the class. Some students who would bravely attempt any physical challenge whatsoever in my other classes would be utterly stymied by the idea of improvisation, of coloring outside the lines. They were so used to being told exactly what to do — and being "successful" at it — that wide-open windows of freedom paralyzed them. They were exiting their comfort zone and risked being awkward and graceless. Simply put, they were so focused on "Getting It Right" that not only had they lost the joy of exploring, but they were also stumped when asked to be even marginally creative or playful.

Dogs never have this problem. Belle, as a very obedient dog, happily follows by my side on long walks. Yet in the time it takes me to unfasten her leash, she can instantly switch into Playtime Mode completely, plunging into a madcap tug-of-war over an empty Evian bottle with Dwayne or a mock tussle with Dingo.

For her, Playtime is always just a breath or two away — exactly where it should be for all of us if we practice the secret of **STAYING CURIOUS**.

THE ADVANTAGES OF BEING AN OMNIVORE

As with all Labs, Belle's appetite is inexhaustible. She's pretty much never met a snack or a meal she hasn't happily devoured. In short, she is NOT a picky eater.

On the other hand, as a yoga teacher and a city slicker, I am surrounded by an enormous range of people with major food obsessions and restrictions.

Alongside every variety of weight-loss diet (Atkins, Scarsdale, South Beach, Zone, and dozens more), I have friends who are raw foodists, unwilling to eat anything cooked above 104 degrees. I know wine and food connoisseurs who are constantly exploring the fanciest, most exotic, and trendiest restaurants. And I've got many friends who love fasting — everything from the Master Cleanse to juice fasts and colonics. I even have strict vegan friends who won't touch vegetables or pasta if there's a chance the dish might have brushed up against some meat in the kitchen — guilt by association!

Without judging anyone's dietary preferences, it's still pretty clear that we are so wildly picky about the food we eat (and the cars we drive and the clothes we wear), and yet we are hardly choosy at all about our thoughts. Students in my meditation workshops always report that they feel their thoughts are thinking them, rather than the other way around. We are, more or less, people who passionately scrutinize clothing labels and menus, while setting our brains on "default."

I certainly share this experience. So often, my thoughts feel like they're "just happening," almost as though I've walked into a room with the radio on and I'm totally unable to change the station or the volume. I'm stuck listening to music I'm really not that into, yet I never realize that I might have the power to change stations or just turn the radio off.

Belle, on the other hand, absolutely demonstrates the ability to select her focus. Coming into my office today, she accidentally got bumped by the door and let out a quick yelp that startled me. She ran inside immediately, however, instantly in search of her favorite toy.

I'm pretty sure that if it had been me, I probably would have stood there for a moment complaining. I might have tried to get sympathy from whoever was around. Or, worse still, I might have woven the event into some self-fulfilling narrative about how I was having a bad day already. Belle, realizing there were many playtoys in her immediate vicinity, charged forward fully focused on how much fun she could be having right now.

In my life, I've seen a handful of people completely transform themselves through radical changes in diet. I've seen fewer people transforms themselves with sweeping or profound changes in their thoughts, but when I have it's breathtaking.

Much more than "You are what you eat," yoga teaches us that we are what we think. We have to get authentically curious about all those thoughts we take as a given, becoming interested in what's really going on inside our heads. Belle's a terrific reminder that if we directed a fraction of the fussiness we extend to other areas of our lives (diet, clothing, and cars etc.) to being discriminating about the thoughts we allow to live in our brains, our transformation might just be a miracle.

SECRET #7
LET GO
How Belle maintains her constant state of frolicsome freedom and spiritual alignment

FETCH

As a pureblooded retriever, Belle — thanks to generations of disciplined breeding — is genetically-programmed to passionately love chasing after things. With her over-the-moon love of Frisbees, balls, and sticks, she expresses a deeply-ingrained part of her DNA that required no real teaching on my part. What impresses me most, however, is her letting go of her prize.

After she's captured her trophy, Belle runs right back to me full of pride. Loving the chase and excited about her victory, she must find it counterintuitive to release the triumphant prize immediately after she's seized it. Even now, if I don't specifically say "Let Go" she'll try to initiate a friendly tug of war with me, much like she does with her puppy friends Dwayne and Dingo.

As soon as I say "Let Go," however, Belle prances up and down, supremely eager for the next round. She is instantly at the ready, running a few feet ahead of me, alternating her gaze by focusing alternately on my throwing arm and the distance before her. Completely eager to bolt and begin her new quest, she somehow knows and accepts that one must "let go" if the game is to continue.

When we lived in Vancouver, we were five minutes away from the dog beach in the heart of the city. This was Belle's idea of Nirvana.

And of course, she couldn't understand why we would ever want to leave the beach. Fully living the secret HAVE FUN — and since retrieving a Frisbee in the water is for her the ultimate expression of fun — she never wanted it to end.

Every time we started to walk away, she kept leaping for the Frisbee in my hand. She would look at me incredulously, more or less asking "Why in God's name are we stopping?" Although Belle's forever rooted in the present, she really did not want to let go of such a peak moment.

I hit upon an easy solution that somehow worked. I simply put the Frisbee in my backpack. As soon as I zipped it up, with the Frisbee out of sight, she accepted we were leaving and took her place by my side.

Belle is smart enough to remember pretty much everything that's of interest to her. On our walks, she commits to memory every store clerk or other individual who have ever given her a treat. Months later, she will make a beeline towards all remembered sources of food.

So often we're unwilling to risk releasing what we're clinging to, essentially ensuring that we stay stuck.

Belle certainly didn't forget about the Frisbee or think it didn't exist anymore. Having the Frisbee out of sight was merely a clear signal to her that this particular adventure was over. It simply allowed her to "let go" of it in the present moment. In this case, "out of sight" really did equal "out of mind."

What if we humans had that discipline? How great would it be if all those ex-boyfriends and ex-girlfriends and financial worries and career concerns could vanish from our thoughts simply by our putting them "out of sight." So often, however, we're unwilling to risk releasing what we're clinging to, essentially ensuring that we stay stuck.

One of my all-time favorite quotes from Winston Churchill is this one: **"Success is the ability to go from failure to failure without losing enthusiasm."**

While in Belle's case, success is really about the ability to transition from one happy romp to another, it's still pretty much the same point.

Whether one has experienced a success or a failure, letting go is really about the ability to move forward with enthusiasm. It's an active choice. All we have to do is let the Frisbee rest inside the bag and decide to think about something else. As Belle demonstrates, it's really about our ability to keep looking at life with joyful expectancy, asking over and over again, "OK, that's over…What's next?"

SEEK THE SHADE

Belle and I have our hiking routine down to a science.

Arriving at Runyon Canyon, we travel the basic route counter-clockwise, playing Fetch from the moment I let her off-leash. As always, her enthusiasm is unbounded.

This continues as we pass the first water station, where she grabs a drink (and tries to dog-paddle manically in the bowl.) We resume Fetch until the ascent begins to get more dramatic. At that point, Belle makes a decision. Still holding her stick, she runs ahead of me to find a shady patch — even if it means going off the trail a bit and waiting under the bushes — and she waits for me. After

I pass her, she runs on ahead once again to seek out another spot of shade. Once we're at the summit however, we run down together, pretty much keeping perfect pace with each other (unless I need to stop and re-tie my sneakers) until we're ground-level once again.

I love Belle's self-pacing on our journey. She treasures her exuberant rounds of Fetch at the beginning, but as the climb gets steeper — and knowing there's a 10 minute run at the end — she makes a set of smart decisions to rest in the shade.

Under the hot desert sun, she feels no need to continue until heat exhaustion sets in. I certainly did not train her to seek out a shady patch and wait for me to approach. There's just nothing masochistic or self-sacrificing about my dog.

In yoga class, we teachers feel obliged to say, "If ever you need a rest, please take Child's Pose" but I often believe that students think that's a kind of "wimping out." Students sometimes confide to me that they often feel obliged to push their limits and not take a break unless they are injured or truly exhausted. Unlike Belle, who has the good sense to take a break whenever she can, we humans somehow think that a little rest is an indication of weakness, or worse, failure.

I used to feel the same, thinking that if I could do a pose, I should do the pose. I felt the need to perform, as though the teacher were a drill sergeant and I were required to do everything asked of me, or as if I were in the Olympics and had to win the gold. Knowing I'd survive, I would always tough it out.

I've learned a lot from Belle's deliberately choosing to be in the shade. Now when I take someone's class —

although I always follow the directions as a sign of respect for the teacher and a desire to be part of the unity of the room — I never feel the need to push myself to prove anything. In fact, even if I can totally do

Action can create so much resistance that we never achieve the goal we're striving so valiantly towards.

it, I sometimes opt out of the hardest variation offered, exploring the gentler options instead.

I've learned that letting go — you might also call it "allowing" or "surrender" — is often so much more effective than action alone. Action can create so much resistance that we never achieve the goal we're striving so valiantly towards.

We've all heard story after story of people who relaxed their grip on something, who stopped charging relentlessly ahead, and only then succeeded. Whether it's the couple who stop trying to conceive and then instantly get pregnant, or the individual who after a long unemployment gets five job offers all in a row, there's a magic that comes with letting go of resistance.

On our hikes, Belle models this for me perfectly. Knowing exactly when to act and when to allow, our journey culminates in a light-hearted duet downhill together, both of us running happily and completely in synch.

FETCH AND FORGIVENESS

Each and every time Belle lets go when we play Fetch, I am struck by how happy she is in the moment of release. There's sheer joy that another round has begun, happiness that can only come from surrender.

It's often said that all of yoga philosophy can be summarized as "Letting Go." Whether it's about clinging to the past, worrying about the future, or getting attached to fleeting desires, we have to let go to find the happiness we seek. Perhaps the most powerful form of letting go we can experience comes through forgiveness.

A few years ago I co-created and directed a play called *Miracle In Rwanda* with my wonderful friend Leslie Lewis Sword that's been touring the world to great acclaim. At this writing it's played more than 150 performances over five continents and is still moving audiences to tears and thunderous applause.

Miracle In Rwanda tells the story of Immaculée Ilibagiza. Immaculée's family was brutally murdered during the slaughter that began in Rwanda in April of 1994 when over 1 million people were killed in just three months. Amazingly, for 91 days, Immaculée and seven other women huddled silently and cramped together in an undiscovered extra bathroom — one with a floor that was only two feet wide by three feet long! — in a local pastor's home. Years later when *Sixty Minutes* profiled Immaculée, she and the other survivors returned to this very site, barely able to fit standing together in this tiny space.

In the course of our play, Leslie Lewis Sword brilliantly depicts our friend Immaculée experiencing the entire range of human emotions. Her terror escalates as literally hundreds of machete-wielding killers search the house where she is hiding again and again. Calling out her name, they are determined to find and butcher her as they have all the other members of her family. Immaculée moves beyond her intense fear into rage and despair, somehow in the end managing to find a deeper spiritual connection than she ever thought possible.

Immaculée is often called "our generation's Anne Frank" — yet one who thankfully survived a holocaust. I believe that the true miracle of her story is her ability to choose her spiritual focus and to let go. Astonishingly, she somehow manages to find it within herself to forgive even those who had murdered her own mother and father and brothers.

The facts of Immaculée's story are so incredible — the brutality of the murders and the squalor of her conditions — that countless audience members have had the same response: if she can forgive something that horrible, maybe I can forgive someone I haven't been able to forgive in my own life. Almost all our injustices and grievances pale in comparison, allowing her journey to inspire our possibilities.

Interestingly, Immaculée is very clear that one of the primary motivations behind her remarkable attitude is not some kind of theoretical, saintly altruism, but rather the fact that forgiveness simply feels better than holding on to rage and hatred. Paradoxically, letting go is the most self-serving option you can exercise because it's the only way to truly free yourself from your own misery.

I've observed so many people in my own life — including myself — who may have gone through a wrenching break-up or a divorce, but for a long time still had not let go of the past. The ink might have dried on the legal papers long ago, and every trace of the ex may have been removed from the visible environment, yet inside the battle continues far longer, unabated. I've also known colleagues who've quit their jobs and traveled to India, yet still maintained the same level of resentment they had felt at their former bosses, just as if they were still only working a cubicle away. Time and geography may

It's so tempting to hold on and rehash old subjects endlessly, but it completely prevents new conversations from arising and fresh ideas from flowing.

soften things a bit, but the heart must truly let go in order to be free. Otherwise, you're stuck in an endless tug of war, never to enjoy the next round that life wants to offer you.

Every day there's a constant barrage of little things — "atrocities" like unreturned phone calls and emails, the bad service at the local bistro, the neighbor's overnight guest who steals my parking spot — that require daily moments of letting go anew. It's so tempting to hold on and rehash old subjects endlessly, but however temporarily satisfying that seems, it completely prevents new conversations from arising and fresh ideas from flowing.

In the most practical way, every sunny day while playing Fetch, Belle teaches me that you've just got to let go of the Frisbee if you want another chance to chase after it. If she's willing to let go of something she treasures so much, I need to be willing to let go of anything that is negative and holding me back. You can't cling to the past and simultaneously participate in life's next adventure.

And if you're lucky enough to witness Belle's joy in an endless cycle of letting go during Fetch, trust me: you'll need no further proof that the letting go is indeed truly tremendous.

PLAYING DEAD

Winston Churchill was once asked, "To what do you attribute your success in life?"

He said without hesitating: **'Economy of effort. Never stand up when you can sit down, and never sit down when you can lie down.'**

I taught a private yoga lesson recently at a fancy Los Angeles hotel. We worked in the deluxe gym area. When it came time for the final rest (*savasana* or corpse pose), because the gym was only semi-deserted, I asked my student if she'd be comfortable lying down and practicing corpse pose here.

"Oh, I can take a nap anywhere," she cheerfully replied. "It's one of my favorite things about myself!"

I really loved that. Not only did my student have a favorite thing about herself, but also that she was willing to explore this pose in an unusual environment, especially since *savasana* is traditionally said to be the most difficult of all the yoga poses.

At the end of almost every yoga class, one practices corpse pose by lying down, closing one's eyes, and relaxing all the limbs. You are sometimes directed to scan the body for physical tension of any kind and encouraged to willingly release it. While *savasana* is not technically napping, speaking strictly off the record, it's pretty close. You more or less practice giving up control — of the body, but especially of the mind — and that's why for most yoga students this truly is the most challenging pose of all.

I can't tell you the number of wonderful Type A New Yorkers I've taught who would rather suffer through a thousand extra push-ups than lie still for ten minutes. I also know gifted yoga teachers who are geniuses at physical movement, but feel trapped and frustrated by having to "just lie there." I even have a dear teacher friend who swears she cannot nap no matter how tired she is or how much she wants to because her daytime mind will not stop racing a-mile-a-minute with all she has to accomplish.

Belle, on the other hand, is a superb napper. She has no trouble letting go whenever she can, diving straight into the refreshing pool of pure positive energy that is sleeping.

Practicing corpse pose, we are also preparing in some ways for the ultimate letting-go experience: our own death.

While many would view this as depressing and frightening, everything in yoga philosophy continually reminds us of our true spiritual nature. Over and over, the sacred texts tell us of our cosmic connection, that we are temporary expressions of the Infinite. Death merely means we dissolve back into Bliss.

Don't get me wrong: I fully believe in the eternalness of Spirit, but if there were a pill that would allow Belle's lifespan to exist as long as mine, I'd sell everything I own to buy it. I don't like to think about what the world would be like without her constantly by my side.

And yet, I do take comfort from a narrative passed around the Internet recently about a six year-old named Shane and how he accepted the death of a beloved dog, Belker.

"We sat together for a while after Belker's Death, wondering aloud about the sad fact that animal lives are shorter than human lives. Shane, who had been listening quietly, piped up, 'I know why'.

Startled, we all turned to him. What came out of his mouth next stunned me. I'd never heard a more comforting explanation. It has changed the way I try and live.

He said, 'People are born so that they can learn how to live a good life — like loving everybody all the time and being nice, right?' The six-year-old continued, 'Well, dogs already know how to do that, so they don't have to stay as long.' "

Truly, Belle knows how to live an awesome life. More than anyone I've studied with or any book I've ever read, every day Belle teaches me how to live simply, to care deeply, to love generously, and to enjoy every moment of my life.

And while I hope she'll be around forever, my little chocolate lab, my greatest teacher, has already more than done her job.

I only hope that sharing her secrets for an awesome life brings you half the joy that Belle herself has brought me....

ACKNOWLEDGMENTS

If Belle has taught me anything, it's to thrive on the joy that comes from appreciating those around me. Even though Belle is the most loyal and helpful being I know, there are so many human individuals who come quite close in their unwavering level of support.

Leslie Lewis Sword for always being my first reader, for the oceanic level of her encouragement, belief, and enthusiasm, and for the joy of our friendship.

Laura Grey — an amazing designer — and (aside from her beloved "Papa") — the cutest person in the world.

Rebecca Gradinger for championing various incarnations of this project, for insightful creative advice, and for sustaining a belief in my work that is truly invaluable. (And thanks to Dawn Davis for introducing us.)

Jude English for being — next to Belle — not only the most even-keeled individual I have ever met, but also in every way an astonishingly good friend.

My little sister, Carol Krenecky, who gave me Belle on a perfect day in May, a gift that forever changed my life. (And Jeff Capodanno who drove us there and home to NYC.)

Ingrid Von Burg for being a true international angel.

Marie Carter, Josh Schrei, Emily Stone, Tevis Trower, Stephanie Wayland, and especially Katey Lang who read drafts of the proposal and manuscript.

Julie Hilden for an incredible job of proofreading the manuscript, one typical of her extraordinary generosity.

Kim Dilts for helping get Belle to her first audition and for shooting me upside down.

Susan Ainsworth for her wisdom and friendship.

Stephen Bittrich for web design above and beyond the call.

Eileen Galindo for our Tamarind cottage where this work began and Mya Stark and the Mastodon Mesa Gallery in the Pacific Design Center, perhaps the nicest writer's space in the world to complete this book.

Belle's most intimate fan club, those who've watched her for me during yoga retreats, business trips and vacations: Gro Christensen, Julio Robledo, Tamer Hasan & Katey Lang, Roger Gonzalez, Jennifer Grims, Michael Din, Dan Segan, Michael Bongiorno, and Marie Carter.

June Rose O'Connor English for her Facebook enthusiasm.

The humans behind some of Belle's best friends: Anthony Dupray and Jack, the world's other cutest puppy, Matt Hechinger, owner of Dingo, and Elaine Winter and Nick O'Han, owner of Dwayne.

Zummy Molina for being a perfect hiking buddy for Belle and me.

Shaun Earl who has gotten me through many a trying moment via the wonder of great massage.

Gonca Gul and Ula Sport for a sensational yoga wardrobe for the book tour.

Key friends in the yoga world with whom I've taken and taught endless classes, shared retreats, and just had fun: Bryn Chrisman, Cristy Candler, Lisa Arzt, Nicky Dawda, Mary Dana Abbott, Adam David, Chrissy Wallo, Jennifer Grims, Kiley Holliday, Keely Garfield, Brandin Steffensen, Carrie McCully, Gabriella Barnstone, Terrence McNally, and Glenn Riis.

The angels of my art career, Devon Fleming, Marilyn Garber, Rick Castro and the Antebellum Gallery, Kipton Cronkite, Jennifer Bell, Sharon Hwang, Kyle Clarkson, Alisa Burket, and Matt Michaelsen.

Adrian Pineiro for sharing the most magical autumn ever with me and Belle in beautiful Vancouver.

And the following folks, forever on my speed dial, who helped simply by being there or enriching some other aspect of my life while I crafted this book: My parents and siblings, nieces and nephews, Amy Adler, Hillary Kelleher, Alan De Valle, Atty Phleger, Montgomery Maguire and Elizabeth Few, Genevieve Lynch, Harry Hjardemaal, Fred Kaufman, Katherine C.H.E., Colin Weil, Havona Madama, and Patricia Scanlon.

I'd like to thank some of the wonderful teachers on my spiritual path.

In the world of yoga, I have to single out Dana Flynn and Jasmine Tarkeshi, with whom I did my official yoga certification training at the Laughing Lotus in NYC. They provided such a fantastic education, and for a decade, a joyous yoga home base for me.

In addition, among many other spiritual teachers, I want to acknowledge again those I've quoted or mentioned in this work: Jack Kornfield, Sharon Salzberg, Eric Schiffman, Swami Satchidananda, B.K.S. Iyengar, Yogi Bhajan, A.H. Almaas, and Mihaly Csíkszentmihályi. For many years, I have been continually inspired by the translations of Rumi by Coleman Barks and Hafiz by Daniel Ladinsky.

In particular, I also want to single out Esther and Jerry Hicks for bringing forth the teachings of Abraham to the world. Except, of course, for Belle's shining example, I find the Abraham teachings to be the simplest, purest distillation of universal truth I've ever encountered.

Finally, I have to thank the source of my inspiration, my own chocolate guru herself, Belle. I only hope I've succeeded at capturing a fraction of the love and wisdom she radiates.

CREDITS

Cover Photography by chimodu.com
All other photographs by Edward Vilga,
except for shots of Belle on the beach (page 33,
67, 79, and 98) by John Hawkins Gordon
and Belle and Edward upside down (page 39)
by Kimberly Dilts
Graphic design by Laura Grey

A portion of the sales of Upward Dog will be donated to Puppies Behind Bars

Puppies Behind Bars trains inmates to raise service dogs for service members coming home wounded from Iraq and Afghanistan, and explosive detection canines for law enforcement. The puppies live in prison with their "puppy raisers" from the age of eight weeks to eighteen months. As the puppies mature into well-loved, well-behaved dogs, their raisers learn what it means to contribute to society rather than take from it.

PuppiesBehindBars

ABOUT THE AUTHOR

Edward Vilga is a writer and spiritual teacher.
UPWARD DOG is his sixth book.
He is a Yale graduate.
For more information, please visit www.edwardvilga.com

Made in the USA
Lexington, KY
11 March 2016